100
MORE
GREAT
INDIAN
POEMS

Also by Abhay K.

100 Great Indian Poems
CAPITALS
The Seduction of Delhi
The Eight-eyed Lord of Kathmandu

100
MORE
GREAT
INDIAN
POEMS

Edited by
Abhay K.

B L O O M S B U R Y
NEW DELHI • LONDON • OXFORD • NEW YORK • SYDNEY

BLOOMSBURY INDIA
Bloomsbury Publishing India Pvt Ltd
Second Floor, LSC Building No. 4, DDA Complex, Pocket C – 6 & 7,
Vasant Kunj, New Delhi 110070

BLOOMSBURY, BLOOMSBURY INDIA and the Diana logo are
trademarks of Bloomsbury Publishing Plc

First published 2019

ISBN: 978-93-88038-89-8

2 4 6 8 10 9 7 5 3 1

Printed and bound in India by Rajkamal Electric Press, Kundli

To find out more about our authors and books
visit www.bloomsbury.com and sign up for our newsletters

CONTENTS

EDITOR'S NOTE

India has a plethora of languages and each language is endowed with great poems waiting to be discovered, read, discussed and cherished. How does one put together an anthology of poems from so many Indian languages? How does one introduce the gems of Indian poetry to the world?

After editing CAPITALS in 2016 to bring world poetry to India, I wanted to take *rasa* and riches of Indian poetry to the world. I also wanted to bring the focus back to the poem from the poet. This quest gave birth to *100 Great Indian Poems*, which I put together selecting poems from twenty-eight Indian languages, most of them translated into English.

The overwhelming reception *100 Great Indian Poems* received in India and abroad inspired me to come up with *100 More Great Indian Poems* to serve as its companion volume. University of São Paulo has published its Portuguese edition while Autonomous University of Nuevo León, Monterrey, Mexico has published its Spanish edition. Its Nepali, Italian and Russian editions are all set to be published soon. It is for the first time that a poetry anthology from over two dozen Indian languages covering over three thousand years of Indian poetry has been translated and published into several foreign languages.

Its first edition sold out within first few months of its publication. I've been receiving heartwarming messages about the anthology. Commenting upon the selection of poems in *100 Great Indian Poems*, French philosopher Christopher Macann said, 'they are quintessential, always simple, often profound, generously sensuous, occasionally political and frequently funny.' Reviewing the anthology in the *First Post*, Manik Sharma wrote, '*100 Great Indian Poems*, attempts something endearingly unique and preposterously impossible—to merge and collate 3000 years of Indian poetry's history via a hundred of its samplings...' I have tried to do this 'unique and preposterously impossible' task again by selecting 100 more great poems for both connoisseurs and dilettantes of Indian poetry.

I have used the same selection criteria for this anthology that I had for *100 Great Indian Poems*. There is abundance of light, irony,

sensuousness and spirituality in the poems, which are uniquely Indian. Here it is worth asking, what makes a poem an Indian poem? How is it different from an African or Latin American poem? I think the answer lies in smorgasbord of sensibility, landscape, customs, rituals, mythologies these poems concoct and offer, which are uniquely Indian in some way or the other.

India's regional languages have a wealth of great Indian poems which rarely comes out in the absence of good translations. Every poem included in these two anthologies speaks out loud—we need more translations and translators. The translators whose works have been included here are eminent poets themselves with in-depth knowledge of India's regional languages. These anthologies also highlight the achievements of Indian poetry written in English by Indian poets as well as Indian diaspora poets and how they have turned English—once a foreign language, into their own.

Just like its predecessor, *100 More Great Indian Poems* brings forth the richness and diversity of poetry that exists in India's myriad languages and dialects. It offers translation from yet another regional Indian language, the Chakma, and also includes Tibetan poets who were born in India.

With these two anthologies I hope to open a new window to the world of Indian poetry that delights your senses, offering a distinct Indian taste, smell, colour and mood which come from an ancient and unique civilization.

Abhay K.

AFTER THE CURFEW
—Nida Fazli

It is morning
the sky humbly bows
its head to the earth
for children are going to school

Bathing itself in the stream
the sun dons itself
in a turban of spun gold
and stands smiling by the road
for children are going to school

Winds sing out blessings
on verdant green branches
jingles by fragrant flowers
wake up the sleepy paths
the shady peepal from its
corner of the old street
waves out its hands
for children are going to school

Angles of light come out
every trail is sparkling
at this moment
every pore of the earth
throbs like a mother's heart
time sits happily
on a rundown rooftop
flying pigeons in the sky
for children are going to school
children are going to school.

Translated from Urdu by Nirupama Dutt

AGAIN SNOWFALL
—Jiban Namdung

A poet who used to write
Poems of snow
This year went to the capital
To recite the poems of snow
It is not known
When he will return to the hills
Because the snowfall has started again,
Roads are empty
Paths and corners are desolate
Walking down the same roads and paths
The poet had walked to the hot plains
In search of him, a poem has set out alone
In the snowfall this year.

Translated from Nepali by Jas Yonjan 'Pyasi'

A LOVE POEM FROM INDIA: AUTHOR'S CONSENT
—Mahe Jabeen

right then
as poetry happens
he comes and
kisses me

trying to find meter
in the sound of his feet
I close my eyes

youth
engulfs me
thoughts
that were taking shape
lose their way
my poetic images
get mercilessly plundered

an unmasked love
kisses my naked forehead
a touch immersed in my eyes
shines provocatively
on my cheek
a look perches on the curve of my neck
and moves like a breeze

poetry freed from words
entwines us

lips publish the poem
with the author's consent

Translated from Telugu by Velcheru Narayana Rao

ALPHABETS
—Nabaneeta Dev Sen

When night falls
I search for him
I bring him home
I look him in the eye
And I cage
Language.

When day breaks
Once again the world
Wraps around my eyes
And off he flies
Taking each word
That alphabet bird

Translated from Bengali by Nandana Sen

A MARVEL
—Anon

O Poverty
great powers
you have given me
I see
the whole world
and no one sees me

Translated from Sanskrit by W.S. Merwin and J.M. Masson

AND DEATH DEMANDS A LABOR
—Sumita Chakraborty

When it rains in Boston, from each street rises
the smell of sea. So do the faces of the dead.
For my father, I will someday write:
On this day endeth this man, who did all he could
to craft the most intricate fears, this man
whose waking dreams were of breaking the small bones
in the feet of all the world's birds. Father.
You know the stories. You were raised on them.
To end a world, a god dances. To kill a demon,
a goddess turns into one. Almanacs of annihilation
are chronicled in cosmic time. Go on.
Batter everything of mine that you can find.
Find my roe deer with the single antler. Kill him.
Find a girl, or a woman. Display to me her remains
on some unpaved expanse, like road kill
on Kentucky highways, turning from flesh to a
fine sand made of ground bone, under a sun
whose surface reaches temperatures six times hotter
than the finest crematory. On the surface of the earth,
our remains are in unholy concert with the remains
of all who have gone before and all who will follow,
and with all who live. In this way, our ground
resembles a bone house. Search in my body
for my heart, find it doesn't sit gently
where you learned it to be. Thieve in my armory.
Take my saws, take my torches, and drown
my phalanx of bees. Carve into me the words
of the chronicler of hell. Make your very best
catastrophe. My piano plays loud and fast
although my hands are nowhere to be found.
Father, as you well know, I am but a woman.
I believe in neither gods nor goddesses.

I have left my voice up and down the seam
of this country. I, unlike you, need no saws,
or torches. The bees you drowned will come to me
again. Each time you bear your weapons, I,
no more than a woman, grow a new limb.
Each time you use a weapon, my sinews grow
like vines that devour a maple tree.
When I cry, my face becomes the inescapable sea,
and when you drain blood from a creature,
I drink it. On this day this man died,
having always eaten the good food
amid the angry ghosts, having always made
the most overwrought hells.
On this day the moon waxes gibbous
and the moths breed in the old carpets.
On this day from a slit in the ground rises
a girl who does not live long.
On this day to me a lover turns his back
and will not meet my eye.
On this day the faces of the death-marked
are part-willow, part-lion.
On this day has died an artist of ugly tapestries,
and his wares burst into flame.
On this day endeth this man upon who
I hurl the harvest of this ghostly piano,
and on the surface of this exceptional world
the birds have all come to our thresholds,
our windows and our doors, our floorboards,
our attic crannies and underground storerooms,
wires and railroads, tarmacs, highways,
cliffs and oceans, and have all begun to laugh,
a sound like an orange and glittering fire
that originates from places unseen.

English

A NEW WAY OF WAITING
—Shakunt Mathur

Scolded
the old servant
for his usual slowness.
For his mischief
gave a good slap
to my darling son.

To my daughter who'd been playing
gave a dozen hankies to hem.
Ordered
the oldest
to drink more milk.
Washed
all the dirty clothes.

Flipped through a few magazines.
Darned some torn clothes.
Sewed on some new buttons.
Cleaned the machine and oiled it.

Put the cover back on with care.
Took out the half-finished sewing
and repacked it in a different way.
Wiped the cupboards in the kitchen.
Cleaned the spice jars.

And still
he hasn't come home from the office.

Translated from Hindi by Aruna Sitesh and Arlene Zide

AN ASIAN CHILD ENTERS A BRITISH CLASSROOM
—Debjani Chatterjee

Before she stepped into the classroom:
she removed coat, mittens and chunni;
mentally undid her shoes for entry
to a temple of secular mystery.

She also shed her:
language, name, identity;
donned the mask of neat conformity,
prepared for lessons in cultural anonymity.

English

AN INVITATION
—Vallana

Make haste, traveller, be on your way!
These woods are alive with beasts,
it's almost dusk, and you're awfully young
to be travelling on your own.
I can't invite you to stay here—
a young girl like me, home alone.

Transcreated from Sanskrit by Amanda Bell

AN ORANGE
—Jibanananda Das

Once I have left this body
Shall I not return to earth?
Let me come back
On a winter night
As the doleful flesh of a chilled orange
At the bedside of a dying friend

Translated from Bengali by Arunava Sinha

APPARITION ON THE RIVER BANK
—Bhojya Deva

She squeezes her dripping hair
and from that black lightning
a few sparkling drops trickle.
She stretches her arms up and examines
the firmness of her glistening breasts.
A wet, transparent skirt clings to her thighs.
Bending forward, she scans the bank
before emerging out of the river.

Transcreated from Sanskrit by Bill Wolak and Abhay K.

ASHTAVAKRA GITA CH-1

1: Instruction on Self Realization

Janaka said:

1.1 Master,
how is Knowledge to be achieved,
detachment acquired,
liberation attained?

Ashtavakra said:

1.2 To be free,
shun the experiences of the senses
like poison.
Turn your attention to
forgiveness, sincerity, kindness, simplicity, truth.

1.3 You are not earth, water, fire or air.
Nor are you empty space.
Liberation is to know yourself
as Awareness alone—
the Witness of these.

1.4 Abide in Awareness
with no illusion of person.
You will be instantly free and at peace.

1.5 You have no caste or duties.
You are invisible, unattached, formless.
You are the Witness of all things.
Be happy.

1.6 Right and wrong, pleasure and pain,
exist in mind only.
They are not your concern.

You neither do, nor enjoy.
You are free.

1.7   You are the Solitary Witness
of All That Is,
forever free.
Your only bondage is not seeing This.

1.8   The thought: 'I am the doer'
is the bite of a poisonous snake.
To know: 'I do nothing'
is the wisdom of faith.
Be happy.

1.9   A single understanding:
'I am the One Awareness,
consumes all suffering
in the fire of an instant.
Be happy.

1.10 You are unbounded Awareness—
Bliss, Supreme Bliss—
in which the universe appears
like the mirage of a snake in a rope.
Be happy.

1.11 It is true what they say:
'You are what you think.'
If you think you are bound you are bound.
If you think you are free you are free.

1.12 You are Self—the Solitary Witness.
You are perfect, all-pervading, One.
You are free, desireless, forever still.
The universe is but a seeming in You.

1.13 Meditate on this: 'I am Awareness alone—Unity itself.'
Give up the idea that you are separate, a person,
that there is within and without.

1.14 You have long been bound thinking:
'I am a person.'
Let the knowledge: 'I am Awareness alone'
be the sword that frees you.

1.15 You are now and forever
free, luminous, transparent, still.
The practice of meditation
keeps one in bondage.

1.16 You are pure Consciousness—
the substance of the universe.
The universe exists within you.
Don't be small-minded.

1.17 You are unconditioned, changeless, formless.
You are solid, unfathomable, cool.
Desire nothing.
You are Consciousness.

1.18 That which has form is not real.
Only the formless is permanent.
Once this is known,
you will not return to illusion.

1.19 Just as a mirror exists
both within and without
the image reflected,
the Supreme Self exists
both within and without the body.

1.20 Just as the same space exists
both within and without a jar,
the timeless, all-pervasive One
exists as Totality.

Translated from Sanskrit by Bart Marshall

BARDIC STUFF
—Manohar Shetty

Poets are natural-born schizoids
And psychoanalysts
Have no answer to them.

On the surface they appear
As normal as toast and eggs
And mundane as salt.

But something odd is burning
Them up, something in the blood
That does not show up

In clinical tests or before a judicial
Bench or a bevy of angels,
Gods or painted devils.

All the accoutrements
Of riches and success don't
Seem much to them.

Though they nod and smile
Genially, their minds are a
Permanent someplace else.

One half of their world
Is streaked white and blue, the other
Scarred as the moon

Or to use a more earthly
Simile, they're like those
Camels with not one but

Two humps of water
To carry them through
The scorching dunes.

Traditionally their money,
If they have any,
Drains out like a hose pipe

Forgotten in a garden.
It seems endless, this business
Of planting a poem which

May die as a sapling before
They move on to the next
Though no one is listening

Just as no one does to starlings
Or nightingales, hooting owls,
The trumpeting blue whale

Or to the sound of the planet
Grinding slowly on
Its creaking axis.

English

BEGGAR
—Angshuman Kar

Without informing us
sometimes our friends change their numbers
With whatever force we press the green button then
and dial the old number
it does not ring

Sometimes, however, it rings
and an unknown grave voice says
'wrong number'.

Sometimes
it rings and I hear 'hello'...
I think I am talking to my old friend
I keep on talking
ten seconds elapse, twenty seconds
the line does not get disconnected
then, after sometime,
the person who, in a slightly melancholic voice says
'wrong number'
is too a beggar of words
without informing him
his friends too
have changed their numbers!

Translated from Bengali by Dr Ajoy Ranjan Biswas

BIRTHPLACE WITH BURIED STONES
—Meena Alexander

I

In the absence of reliable ghosts I made aria,
Coughing into emptiness, and it came

A west wind from the plains with its arbitrary arsenal:
Torn sails from the Ganga river,

Bits of spurned silk,
Strips of jute to be fashioned into lines,

What words stake—sentence and make-believe,
A lyric summoning.

II

I came into this world in an Allahabad hospital,
Close to a smelly cow pasture.

I was brought to a barracks, with white walls
And corrugated tin roof,

Beside a civil aviation training center.
In World War II officers were docketed there.

I heard the twang of propellers,
Jets pumping hot whorls of air,

Heaven bent,
Blessing my first home.

III

In an open doorway, in half darkness
I see a young woman standing.

Her breasts are swollen with milk.
She is transfixed, staring at a man,

His hair gleaming with sweat,
Trousers rolled up

Stepping off his bicycle,
Mustard bloom catches in his shirt.

I do not know what she says to him,
Or he to her, all that is utterly beyond me.

Their infant once a clot of blood
Is spectral still.

Behind this family are vessels of brass
Dotted with saffron,

The trunk of a mango tree chopped into bits,
Ready to be burnt at the household fire.

IV

Through the portals of that larger chaos,
What we can scarcely conceive of in our minds—

We'd rather think of starry nights with biting flames
Trapped inside tree trunks, a wellspring of desire

Igniting men and gods,
A lava storm where butterflies dance—

Comes bloodletting at the borders,
Severed tongues, riots in the capital,

The unspeakable hurt of history:
So the river Ganga pours into the sea.

V

In aftermath—the elements of vocal awakening:
Crud, spittle, snot, menstrual blistering,

Also infant steps, a child's hunger, a woman's rage
At the entrance to a kitchen,

Her hands picking up vegetable shavings, chicken bones,
Gold tossed from an ancestral keep.

All this flows into me as mottled memory,
Mixed with syllables of sweat, gashed syntax,

Strands of burst bone in river sand,
Beside the buried stones of Sarasvati Koop—

Well of mystic sky-water where swans
Dip their throats and come out dreaming.

English

BUDDHA ON THE HIGHWAY
—Kalpatta Narayanan

Yesterday
I saw Buddha cross the road.
I had been waiting long on this side
unable to cross in the evening rush
thinking how we wait for a year
or a year and a half in order to cross the road
in a life fifty, sixty or seventy years long.

He crossed the road, slow, fearless.
As I began to follow him
a vehicle rushed forward screaming at me.

No vehicle slowed down for him;
he just walked along
a wild, wide, desolate path
which was always there
and reached the other side.

Translated from Malayalam by K. Satchidanandan

CITY OF MEMORIES
—Sunil Gangopadhyay

People at the borders speak prose
In ghettoes and factories they speak prose
During the day the city speaks prose
All contemporary miseries speak prose
The parched field and the rough unkempt men speak prose
The entire civilization of scissors and knives talk prose.
What then shall poetry be about?

Translated from Bengali by Kalyan Roy and Bonnie MacDougall

DARING
—Padma Sachdev

No one drinks from the well
to the right of our hill,
though it brims with bright water;
no one glances that way,
since a calf drowned in its depths,
deceived by drifting blossoms.
Deep in its core, shadows yearn
for their return—the girls with vessels.
The water calls to me in daylight,
implores me to imbibe it
in full sight. At night, I bathe
unseen in its darkness, cup
its coolness in my palms
and raise it to my mouth—
my thirst is as insatiable as love.

Transcreated from Dogri by Amanda Bell

DAY AFTER DAY
—Annamaya

Life, day after day, is a game
To find what you cannot see
    is truth.
Coming is real. Going is real.
What you do in between is a game.
Right in front of you
lies the world.
At the very end
is truth.
We eat food. We wear clothes.
It's all part of this passing game.
The past clings to our bodies.
Cross the doorway:
there is truth.
Badness never ends,
and there's never enough good.
In the end, time is a game.
High on the mountain, God is king.
Higher than heaven
is truth.

*Translated from Telugu by Velcheru Narayana Rao and
David Shulman*

DECEPTION
—Sampurna Chattarji

everything seems to glide and dance
in synchronicity the trains come and go sliding
past each other
the motor boats appear at the same spot
the birds sink towards the tracks
the light moves
people walk into the light
the most secret god is a clock

English

DO NOT ASK
—H.S. Shivaprakash

Do not ask me who brought water
Into the blazing midday's silence
Do not ask who brought me light
Into my prison in netherworlds

Do not ask who brought cooling breeze
To the pyre-ridden cremation ground
Do not ask me who brought a poem
To the market's din and bustle

Do not ask me who brought the spring
To my land wrecked with famines
Do not say: Shiva Prakash. Not me,
But it is you, you and you alone

Translated from Kannada by the poet

DOTHEAD
—Amit Majmudar

Well yes, I said, my mother wears a dot.
I know they said 'third eye' in class, but it's not
an *eye* eye, not like that. It's not some freak
third eye that opens on your forehead like
on some Chernobyl baby. What it means
is, what it's *showing* is, there's this unseen
eye, on the inside. And she's marking it.
It's how the X that says where treasure's at
is not the treasure, but as good as treasure.—
All right. What I said wasn't half so measured.
In fact, I didn't say a thing. Their laughter
had made my mouth go dry. Lunch was after
World History; that week was India—myths,
caste system, suttee, all the Greatest Hits.
The white kids I was sitting with were friends,
at least as I defined a friend back then.
So wait, said Nick, does *your* mom wear a dot?
I nodded, and I caught a smirk on Todd—
She wear it to the shower? And to bed?—
while Jesse sucked his chocolate milk and Brad
was getting ready for another stab.
I said, Hand me that ketchup packet there.
And Nick said, What? I snatched it, twitched the tear,
and squeezed a dollop on my thumb and worked
circles till the red planet entered the house of war
and on my forehead for the world to see
my third eye burned those schoolboys in their seats,
their flesh in little puddles underneath,
pale pools where Nataraja cooled his feet.

English

EPITAPH
—Mohammad Alvi

As soon as I reached the grave
I stretched my limbs to rest
thinking no one would disturb me now,
these two yards of land are mine alone
and so I kept turning into soil
losing count of time
but soon my peace was disturbed
somebody else entered my grave
and his epitaph
is carved on my stone.

Translated from Urdu by Anisur Rahman

EXILE

—Ravi Shankar

There's nowhere else I'd rather not be than here,
But here I am, nonetheless, dispossessed,
Though not quite, because I never owned
What's been taken from me, never have belonged
In and to a place, a people, a common history.
Even as a child when I was slurred in school -
Towel head, dot boy, camel jockey -
None of the abuse was precise: only Sikhs
Wear turbans, widows and young girls bindis,
Not one species of camel is indigenous to India . . .
If, as Simone Weil writes, to be rooted
Is the most important and least recognized need
Of the human soul, behold: I am an epiphyte.
I conjure sustenance from thin air and the smell
Of both camphor and meatloaf equally repel me.
I've worn a lungi pulled between my legs,
Done designer drugs while subwoofers throbbed,
Sipped masala chai steaming from a tin cup,
Driven a Dodge across the Verrazano in rush hour,
And always to some degree felt extraneous,
Like a meteorite happened upon bingo night.
This alien feeling, honed in aloneness to an edge,
Uses me to carve an appropriate mask each morning.
I'm still unsure what effect it has on my soul.

English

EYES
—Vasant Abaji Dahake

A night like opium
when the moonlight moans through the water,
that's how your eyes

brim over my face.

Translated from Marathi by Ranjit Hoskote

FAREWELL
—Jiban Narah

On the day our sister departed
she left an unbearable emptiness in her wake.
Because she loved to sing alone
a room of her own was built.
The sad resonance of her singing
scattered in the room—
it hurts us still from time to time.
She left us forever
with the boy she loved—that's the custom,
not easy to accept.
Because she loved the *simalu* blossom
she never told a lie to the river.
The day she sailed downstream
her sorrow began to grow.

Simalu: Silk-cotton tree

Translated from Assamese by Lyra Neog

FOREST BALLADS
—Niranjan Chakma

After each devastating storm
a silence descends on the entire hill.
Distraught birds are puzzled!
Should they return to their shattered nests
or go out in search of food?
One fine morning the birds are afflicted
with an identity crisis.
The name currently used to spot them
had never been heard by them before.

Recently a huge debate about their identity and rights
rocked a scholarly Geneva conference.
References were copiously made to the Vedas.
Stale, century-old theories of the expansionists
were presented with great gusts.
But these participants
had never tried to understand
the forest ballads.

Translated from Chakma by Udayan Ghosh

FROGS
—Buddhadev Bose

Monsoon rains pour down, and the frogs get delirious
singing like a chorus with loud elated voices.
Today there's nothing to fear: neither drought,
nor shortage of warmth,
neither snake's jaws, nor rocks thrown by mischievous boys.
As the grasses thicken like green clouds,
in the bountiful flooded fields
their fleeting splash of immortality echoes louder and louder
with every leap.
They have no necks, but their throats bulge and resonate,
and what smooth bodies, what eyes like cold gemstones—
eyes gazing upwards, unwavering in meditation,
ecstatic, lidless, like the eyes of holy men fixed on God.
The rain comes to an end; the shadows tilt.
Their songs drift like hymns in the expectant air.
Now daylight vanishes silently, but a solemn murmur
stings the twilight, and the translucent sky bends down to hear.
Night and rain, and we're cozy in bed.
Only a single incessant melody resonates through our sleep
like the final lines of a mystic incantation—
the last frog's frenetic croaking, croaking, croaking.

Transcreated from Bengali by Bill Wolak

GIRLS ON ROOFTOPS
—Alok Dhanwa

Still the girls come on to the rooftops
Their shadows fall on my life

The girls are here for the boys
Downstairs, amidst bullets, the boys play cards
Sitting, on the stairs above the drain
Lazing on benches outside the footpath tea-stall
Sipping tea
Around a boy who plays the mouth-organ sweet
Timeless tunes of *Awara, Sree 420.*

A *newspaperwallah* spreads his wares
And some young men read the early edition
Not all are students
Some unemployed yet, small timers some
Whilers, lumpens

But in their veins, bloodstreams
They await a girl
A hope—that from these houses and rooftops
One day, some day—love will arrive.

Awara, Sree 420: popular Hindi films
Newspaperwallah: Someone who delivers newspapers door to door

Translated from Hindi by the poet

GOD

—Anuradha Mahapatra

I've never seen God, but when I notice temples,
I think of Hiranyakashypu, the demon king,
and when I watch a statue worshipped
I think about someone's daughter
being sold for cash. One vanishing life offered to another.
But to see blood coughed from the mouths of the bloodless
is the ultimate joke.

Still, when I spotted that guy
in the filthy blue t-shirt on the train,
stiff as a cast-iron cannon, I wished he were God!
Then at least I could have found a safe hiding place,
or I could have attacked him,
but even if I'd murdered him,
it would have been an act of love.
Nowadays, even when I step onto the bus
I'm thinking about God.

Transcreated from Bengali by Bill Wolak

HERE COMES GOD
—Tenetti Suri

Hey, here comes god,
lifeless in bronze,
parading the streets,
riding his wooden horse.

Ask him about wages, fellows.
Tell him we don't have
enough to eat.

The wise men tell us
even stone hearts melt.
Let's see if that's true.

Bow down to him,
see if he listens,
and let go if he doesn't answer.

Hold up your hands
millions at once
raise your voice
so the sky itself shivers.

Ask him about the wages, fellows.
Tell him we don't have
enough to eat.

Translated from Telugu by Velcheru Narayan Rao

HISTORY OF JUSTICE
—Rohan Chhetri

Some kids from the neighbourhood are bursting firecrackers
by the side of our compound wall. Grandmother is
screaming at them. Mother smiles knowing
they won't listen. Grandfather once stayed up
late in the night at the window of the first floor
waiting for the drunk who pissed on our wall
every night, so he could slosh a good whole bucket
of cold water over his head in the frosty winter night.
He's been dead since long, our grandfather.
But grandmother hasn't forgotten the battered face
of the man who was tied to a post outside the house
for having beaten his wife to a pulp. And grandfather
lunging his fists on the poor man's face. Grandmother
by the window thinking if she had married a monster.
Most of all, the face of her young husband during the time
of the revolution when she went to see him in the lockup,
where he was hung naked upside down for two days,
with mud shoved in his mouth by the Bengali Inspector who
kept saying, *Feed him the land, that's what they are fighting for*

English

HOW CAN A RIVER REJECT ITS FISH?
—Janabai

If the Ganga empties into the sea
and the sea abandons her,
tell me, Vitthal, who would
hear her complaint?

How can a river reject its fish?
How can a mother desert her child?
Jana says, Lord,
accept those who surrender.

Transcreated from Marathi by Bill Wolak

ICE CUBES, CAKE & ROTI
—Souvik Bandopadhyay

On the first peg, Camus, Kafka, Sartre and Foucault
on the second peg, Dante, Neruda, Ginsberg and Picasso
on the third, Freud, Marx, Mayakovsky and Daniken—
    mixing them with ice cubes,
    sipping luxuriously,
    not noticing,
    when had the clock struck midnight.

But we had noted,
that, in his house, he has two dogs,
two servants, and a full moon,
and the dogs eat cake,
while, the servants, burnt *roti*.

Roti: Bread

Translated from Bengali by Neelav Bose

I HAVE BROUGHT THE SACRIFICIAL GOAT
—Joy Goswami

Place the greens below the mound
I have brought the sacrificial animal, a goat

He has forgotten his previous beheading
Yet the mark remains
    Garland-like round his throat

Translated from Bengali by Sampurna Chattarji

IMAGINARY NUMBER
—Vijay Seshadri

The mountain that remains when the universe is destroyed
is not big and is not small.
Big and small are

comparative categories, and to what
could the mountain that remains when the universe is destroyed
be compared?

Consciousness observes and is appeased.
The soul scrambles across the screes.
The soul,

like the square root of minus 1,
is an impossibility that has its uses.

English

INCURABLE
—Yaquin

I desire the door-sill of my beloved
    More than a king's house;
I desire the shadow of the wall where her beauty hides
    More than the Delhi palaces.
Why did you wait till spring;
Were not my hands already full of red-thorned roses?
    My heart is yours,
So that I know not which heart I hear sighing:
    Yaquin, Yaquin, Yaquin, foolish Yaquin.

Translated from Urdu by Edward Powys Mathers

IN THE DUST FOREVER
—Tarannum Riyaz

The winds will dance through the trees
Birds will sing to the gardens
Water will flow into the rivers
Dew drops will fall onto the grass
Evening orange will dissolve the peaks
Boys will play, run through the fields
Juliets will meet their Romeos
Mothers will sing to their children, lullabies
A fistful of ashes of my existence
Will be lost in the dust forever.

Translated from Urdu by Miraan Punjabi

IN THE EVENT OF CHANGE
—Tsering Wangmo Dhompa

I am saying primroses lined the pathway of toothless hedges.

I am saying the ocean shimmered like corrugated steel in the morning sun.

The context of my story changes when you enter. Then I am dung on the wall of the nomad's field. Then the everyday waking person.

I am nodding in your direction like fissures between dandelion fur. Seeing in your manner.

I am speaking your pace. Slippage of silk slippers.

I say you are losing sight. I say your breasts are dry shells.

I am afraid of what I am capable of doing.

This is all a manner of stating how I prepare myself to be loved.

English

I WEAR MY WORDLESSNESS
—K. Srilata

I wear my wordlessness
like a tattered dress,
its stitches undone.
Twice a week,
I wash myself,
dress and all,
in a river of drowning words
in whose lungs,
the despair of poets
has long since settled.
And yet,
this!
a new-born fawn of a poem
taking its first steps.

English

JAISALMER – IV
—Gulammohamed Sheikh

The sun's twelve faces
blazed
and setting
froze
all the twelve worlds.
The orphaned sand just lay there,
and the clouds ran away, seeing their chance.
The stars grinned, impotent
when
all those houses on the desert's
edge
got up and left,
dead camels on their backs;
bundles and belongings
fell useless in the sand,
the riders' turbans flew in
shreds
like the feathers of birds
quite killed and eaten,
and
half-naked men
kept gulping
the desert's thorny air,
their mouths wide open.

Translated from Gujarati by the author and Adil Jussawalla

LET LOOSE THE STINGING BEES
—Kanji Patel

High the hills and high the *mahua* trees
O Birsa's folk

From the *mahuas* rises the sound of the leading *dhol*
Awaken your sleeping *nagadas*
O Birsa's folk
Gather all the Bhils of the hills
Range together the Bhils of the hills
O Birsa's folk
Do a count of the Bhils
O Birsa's folk
Twelve crores and thirty two lakhs
Count the years
O Birsa's folk
A lakh of moons and a crore of suns

The bullets rain from all directions
O Birsa's folk
The cannon balls *angrezi, desi*
Surrounded, in the hills and rivers
O Birsa's folk
Leave the *dhols*, pick up your bows
Surrounded, in the forests and rocks
O Birsa's folk

From the earthen pots
let loose the captured stinging bees

This song is based on a song of the Bhils in the Panchmahals, Gujarat.

The *Mahua* tree (Bassia latifolia or Madhuca latifolia) is considered sacred by the Bhils.
Birsa refers to Birsa Munda, a tribal hero and important figure in the

Indian freedom struggle, leading the tribals of the Chhotanupur region into the struggle. His struggle was not only against the British but an emancipatory struggle of the tribal people against the Zamindars and money lenders exploiting them.

Dhol is a kind of drum.

Nagada is a drum played to announce the beginning of battle.

Translated from Gujarati by Gopika Jadeja

LINEAGE
—Attoor Raviverma

Granddad loved
the Union Jack
with its stripes and squares:
he was a village officer.

Dad hoisted a tricolor.
He was a freedom fighter.

I hold aloft a red flag.

My grandson's hands
hold a Yankee flag
with fifty stars.

Translated from Malayalam by K. Satchidanandan

LOVE IS EVERYDAY NEW AND FRESH
—Bulleh Shah

The day I learnt the lesson of love
I was scared of the mosque.
I looked around and entered a temple
Where many a drum was beaten.
Love is everyday new and fresh.

Tired of reading the Vedas and the Quran,
Kneeling and protesting, my forehead was rubbed off.
God is neither in the Hindu shrine nor at Mecca.
He who has found Him, he is enlightened.
Love is everyday new and fresh.

Burn the prayer mat, break the water pot,
Quit the rosary, throw the staff.
Lovers say at the top of their voice;
'Leave Kosher meat and eat the dead.'
Love is everyday new and fresh.

Heer and Ranjha have already met;
In vain, she looks for him in the orchard.
Ranjha lies in the folds of her arms.
Lost her senses, she has gained them back.
Love is everyday new and fresh.

Translated from Punjabi by K.S. Duggal

MAKING LOVE TO HER
—Dharmakirti

Making love to her lasts only moments
like a dream, illusion, ending in regret
I reflect upon this truth a hundred times
Yet my heart can't forget the gazelle-eyed girl.

Translated from Sanskrit by Abhay K.

MEDITATIONS ON DESIRE
—Saleem Peeradina

1
I can never say
what I feel about you.
Listen hard
for syllables unspoken,
not yet formed.
As for words
that do surface,
frisk them thoroughly
before inviting them in.

3
Only in the abstract
can words attain
such luminosity.
On contact
with the flesh
they burn up.

9
This love
I send up
like a kite
gives the empty sky
something
to hold on to.

English

MOMIN
—Kailash Vajpeyi

There were houses of worship
Earlier too
There were killing fields as well
This is the progress
We have made
Now the two
Are one

Translated from Hindi by Ananya Vajpeyi

MONSOON POEM
—Tishani Doshi

Because this is a monsoon poem
expect to find the words jasmine,
palmyra, Kuruntokai, red; mangoes
in reference to trees or breasts; paddy
fields, peacocks, Kurinji flowers,
flutes; lotus buds guarding love's
furtive routes. Expect to hear a lot
about erotic consummation inferred
by laburnum gyrations and bamboo
syncopations. Listen to the racket
of wide-mouthed frogs and bent-
legged prawns going about their
business of mating while rain falls
and falls on tiled roofs and verandas,
courtyards, pagodas. Because such
a big part of you seeks to understand
this kind of rain—so unlike your cold
rain, austere rain, get-me-the-hell-
out-of-here rain. Rain that can't fathom
how to liberate camphor from the vaults
of the earth. Let me tell you how little
is written of mud, how it sneaks up
like a sleek-gilled vandal to catch hold
of your ankles. Or about the restorative
properties of mosquito blood, dappled
and fried against the wires of a bug-zapping
paddle. So much of monsoon is to do
with being overcome—not from longing
as you might think, but from the sky's
steady bludgeoning, until every leaf
on every unremembered tree gleams
in the abyss of postcoital bliss.

Come. Now sip on your masala tea,
put your lips to the sweet, spicy skin
of it. There's more to see—notice
the dogs who've been fucking on the beach,
locked in embrace like an elongated Anubis,
the crabs scavenging the flesh of a dopey-
eyed ponyfish, the entire delirious coast
with its philtra of beach and saturnine
clouds arched backwards in disbelief.
And the mayflies who swarm in November
with all their ephemeral grandeur to die
in millions at the behest of light, the geckos
stationed on living room walls, cramming
fistfuls of wings in their maws. Notice
how hardly anyone mentions the word
death, even though the fridge leaks
and the sheets have been damp for weeks.
And in this helter-skelter multitude
of gray-greenness, notice how even the rain
begins to feel fatigued. The roads and sewers
have nowhere to go, and like old-fashioned pursuers
they wander and spill their babbling hearts
to electrical poles and creatures with ears.
And what happens later, you might ask,
after we've moved to a place of shelter,
when the cracks in the earth have reappeared?
We dream of wet, of course, of being submerged
in millet stalks, of webbed toes and stalled
clocks and eels in the mouth of a heron.
We forget how unforgivably those old poems
led us to believe that men were mountains,
that the beautiful could never remain
heartbroken, that when the rains arrive
we should be delighted to be taken
in drowning, in devotion.

English

MOUNTAIN CHILD
—Nirmala Putul

The mountain child—
a fragment of the mountain—
plays in the lap of the mountain

Toddling up the mountain
he plants his feet in the mountain soil
to rise like a mountain
in the land of mountains

The whole mountain
lives inside the mountain child
And in the lap of the mountain
lives the scurrying mountain child

The mountain child sees
a plane flying over the mountain
And he asks his father—
What is that bird?

Translated from Hindi by Lucy Rosenstein

MY EIGHT-ANNA COIN
—Vinod Kumar Shukla

My eight-anna coin
Is lost.
When I look for it
I find a silver rupee.
The rupee isn't mine,
But stamped on it
Is my severed head.
The rest of me must then be
In the eight-anna coin,
And that's why I've been
Desperately looking for it.
How was I to know
That my incomplete person
Would turn into
This money chase?

Translated from Hindi by Arvind Krishna Mehrotra

MY SISTER'S BIBLE
—S. Joseph

This is what my sister's Bible has:
a ration-book come loose,
a loan application form,
a card from the cut-throat money-lender,
the notices of feasts
in the church and the temple,
a photograph of my brother's child,
a paper that says how to knit a baby cap,
a hundred-rupee note,
an SSLC book.

This is what my sister's Bible doesn't have:
the preface,
the Old Testament and the New,
maps,
the red cover.

Translated from Malayalam by K. Satchidanandan

NEED
—Ramesh Chandra Shah

Now when everything is according to the season,
the temperature is just what it should be in these days
after a long time, the sky is breathing freely
and there is no one to reprimand the sun
then

why do I feel
as if something very precious
that I had
has been left behind
in that bad weather?
Why is it that for me alone
all directions
cover themselves with dust?
Why have the mountains
gleaming like a mirror till yesterday, turned alien to me?

What do I want, after all?
What is that need
that is neither
the farmer's
nor the potter's?

Translated from Hindi by the poet

NEGRO, MY BROTHER
—Ali Sardar Jafri

In this forest of ivory,
His black body,
Like a swirling black cloud,
Like a flash of black lightening,
A sea of black limbs,
That ebbs and flows and meanders,
Shining in the blazing sun,
Can turn into a spear,
Dancing to the beats of drums,
It takes on the enemy.
Negro, my brother,
Picks flowers from every forest.
My brother's feet are red,
Like roses.

Translated from Urdu by Baider Bakht and Kathleen Grant Jaeger

NIGHT'S GOLDEN WINEGLASSES
—Habba Khatoon

I've dyed my hands with henna.
When will he return to me?
While he roams distant lands, I'm dying—
my heart feels numb.

I've waited so long for him.
Now where's the delight in daylight?
Even night's golden wineglasses
grow dim.

But love's ritual remains sweet.
If only I could adorn my darling
with jewels, perfume his body,
and anoint him with my slippery kisses.

Although I'm torn apart inside,
love, thanks to you,
look across the lake.
That's the lotus of my heart in bloom.

Transcreated from Kashmiri by Abhay K. and Bill Wolak

NO, I AM NOT LOSING MY SLEEP
—Pash

No
I am not losing my sleep over
how and when
you'll strike
to finish me off
frankly, I couldn't care less
about it
because
I don't have the patience
of a watchman
to be on an eternal guard
to sift and filter
countless moments
to wait for
the time slot
your henchman have fixed for me?

No
I don't waste my time thinking about such trifles
nor am I sentimental about
the memories of my village
and the folks I left behind
No I don't think now about
such things as
the fine hues of red
when the sun sets over the village
nor do I care about
how she feels.

Translated from Punjabi by Suresh Sethi

ONLY A CONNOISSEUR
—Anon Baul

Only a connoisseur of the flavours of love can
comprehend the language of a lover's heart
others have no clue.
The taste of lime rests in the core of the fruit,
and even experts know of no easy way to reach it.
Honey is hidden within the lotus bloom—but the
bee knows it.
Dung-beetles nestle in dung, discounting honey.
Submission is the secret of knowledge.

Translated by Anon

ONLY ONE FACE
—Pankaj Chaturvedi

there is a famous statue
of Buddha in Kushinagar

seen from one angle it seems as if
Buddha is smiling
from a second angle he seems
lost in melancholic thoughts
from a third angle there is
the blessing of nirvana—
inviolable peace

do not think of this as the sum
of three expressions
Buddha could not just smile

his smile was melancholic
and in between
the radiance of desirelessness
or of the middle path

great the skill
that sculpted this stone
but greater still
the understanding of this art
which could discern
that in these three images there was
only one face of Buddha

Translated from Hindi by Rahul Soni

PIGEONS
—Bibhu Padhi

They embody a consciousness
that shines among light-grey rocks.
In their bodies old stories of flight
repeat themselves, refresh memory.
During the long Indian afternoons
they rest upon our polished floors,
their bodies refracting the warmth
of close contact, their small heads

forming a community of wisdom.
A picture of extreme importance is seen
a picture that comprehends everything,
all things contemporary and long past.
But before our eyes gain their fixed look
and our envy its pale green stare,
they rise up, holy and untouched,
to disappear in a history
of mocking wings,
in the accepting sky.

English

PORTRAIT

—Dinkar Manwar

Don't turn away from me
Water
Stay within my sight
Don't babble or gush
Be utterly silent
Be utterly still

Let me enter deep into you
Let me at last hear your voice
Let me feel you with my desperate hands
Let my tongue lick your feet
Let me get a sense
Of what all you have been hiding in your heart

Water
My father my mother my lord
Wait for me for a while
I want to paint
Your portrait.

Translated from the Marathi by Sachin Ketkar

PRAYER
—Prabodh Parikh

Grant me the strength to look at you, to bear the radiance
of the sun;
the strength to alert faraway ships by my drumbeats,
to be a pearl diver,
to drive a toy-train,
to survive a famine,
to extract the magic potion from the tresses
of the femme-enfant.
Grant me, once more, an illusion.
And though I am no Socrates,
grant me the vision to hear, to swim
in the currents of the landscapes of French poets
which, half-open, float away in my blood.

Grant me an alphabet
of airplane and city,
which would let me sit by an ageing grandmother.
Grant me, once more, the illusion
of a ladder
to climb to You,
to me.

Translated from Gujarati by Naushil Mehta and Ranjit Hoskote

RĀGHAVAPĀṆḌAVĪYA
—Kaviarāja

1.47

If you have not followed
the paths of poetry,
finding your way through the vines
and shoots of learning;
if the difficulty of word-weaving
is lost on you, with nothing decent to say
about the work of others;
if you haven't spent long hours
in the company of artists and aesthetes
who are you to make fuss
over my poems?

Transcreated from Sanskrit by Gabriel Rosenstock and Abhay K.

RUMI AND THE REED
—Tabish Khair

Listen to the song of the reed flute:
    It sings of separation.
Torn from the leaf-layered, wind-voiced
    Banks of the pond,
It is joined to sorrow and joy
    By a slender sound.
Who, asked Rumi, can understand
    The reed's longing to return?
        Let its raw lips rest then;
        Let all words be brief then.

And I, O Believers, cried Rumi
    (Having lost the man he loved),
I who am not of the East
    Nor of the West, un-Christian,
Not Muslim or Jew, neither
    Born of Adam nor Eve,
What can I love but the world itself,
    What can I kiss but flesh?
        Let my raw lips rest then;
        Let all words be brief.

English

SATYABHAMA

—Basudev Sunani

Satyabhama
Chuckled on the window seat
Of the bus, and then
Hid her face
In her hands

Was she shy?

Satyabhama
Faint, dark, like a slate,
Forgotten.

How could she
Have been otherwise?

It's two decades since
She was in class five
And I in two
In our village school.

On her cheek
The flush of self-confidence
To have learnt by rote
The alphabet.

Married to a dhoti-clad gentleman,
She is now in search
Of a suitable girl
For her son;

Persuaded by the villagers
She is now a candidate
In the local body election;

She said all this
Pressing her face
To the window-sill.

Satyabhama
Gives the feeling
Of someone intimate
Like the torn pages
Of an old book

From childhood

When eating porridge together
She taught me the art
Of sewing sal-leaf bowls.

There was nothing more
To share with Satyabhama.

By the time bus left
It seemed like
I was in class five
And she in class two.

I do not know
If I will meet her again.

If only I had had
A fleeting glimpse
Of her face.

Translated from Odia by Rabindra K. Swain

SHADOW
—Brij Nath Betab

My own shadow
Overshadows my size,
Do I have a size?
I ask myself;

Does a migrant have some size?
I doubt it.

Translated from Kashmiri by the poet

SILHOUETTE
—Adil Jussawala

Ravi asks me to wait, he'll give me a ride.
Delhi is quiet now, he'll give me a ride.
He saw many, taken in trucks, go for a ride.

A man with a face as flat as a hand
steps up and says, Keep Discipline,
Emergency means Discipline,
then falls back silent.

Across the street, on a terrace two stories high,
a silhouette
hits out and runs, hits nothing, runs.

Twenty years later, its feet broken,
will its hands fly to its face when a light's switched on?
Will it lie on a plank for days,
twisting a handkerchief?

It has my best wishes.

I wish it a straighter back, a strong earth,
I wish it a game that won't cripple.

Ravi studies his car-keys and is silent.
Clouds, not far, make a noise
like MiGs flying low.

There's silence, there's pain.

The boy continues his game
of make-believe cricket.

English

SITA'S TEARS
—Udayan Vajpeyi

Father is unhappy if I wander far from home alone. He buys me a cycle but doesn't let me ride it anywhere.

Every other day, grandmother's servant steals money from grandfather. He ignores the theft and concentrates on rowing the boat of his old age.

Mother tries to run the house with very little money. In order to pass journey, she reads *Ramcharitramanas* over and over again.

Then suddenly one day, as Sita sits in the Ashoka forest, the silhouette of father's sick face appears through her tears.

Translated from Hindi by Alok Bhalla

SON TO MOTHER
—Gnanakoothan

Get too chummy with girls
yours ears will dry up, you said.
If you are naughty
God will strike you blind, you said.
When I worried you for things to eat,
It's bad for your tummy, you said
I got you in exchange for a
winnow of bran, you said.
What a lot of lies, Mother, you told me
when I was young!
What made you stop?
Or did you think
I could survive with truth?
Perhaps you thought
lies for grownups were beyond your ken
and left it to the government
to rule by the law.
I don't like it.
Wean me, mother, when you like,
But feed me your lies
for all time.
You don't love me, don't you?

Translated from Tamil by Ashokamitran

SUMMER AFTERNOON
—Vijay Deo Narayan Sahi

In the nearby bamboo grove
    a sudden chirping of birds

Perhaps the fat black cat
    I often saw on the parapet
        its tail upright
            is crossing the drain

Translated from Hindi by Arvind Krishna Mehrotra

TERMS OF SEEING
—E. V. Ramakrishnan

On our way home from school
We often spent hours in that abandoned
Orchard of mango, cashewnut
And tamarind trees, where each season had
Its fruit and each fruit tasted different.

There we raided the hidden hideouts
Of bootleggers, and broke their buried
Mud-pots. The crematorium in the corner
Revealed an occasional roasted vertebra.
Once we went further and discovered

A disused well, and peeped into its
Vaporous depths: the water smelt like freshly
Distilled alcohol. Through the clotted branches
Of close-knit shadows floated white
Turtles with glazed, metallic shells.

Moving with monastic grace, they looked
Knowledgeable, like much travelled witchcraft
Doctors. If they cast a spell, it was
Unintentional. As we bent down, their
Shaven heads rose and met a shaft of sudden

Sunlight at an angle, tilting the sun
Into the sea. Still, the light lingered over the hill
Like an intimate whisper of something
Forbidden. By this time, the terms of seeing
Were reset: the well was watching us now.

Its riveted gaze pierced us and even went
Beyond us. In the dark cornea of the well

The white turtles moved like exposed optic nerves.
And as if a word was spoken, we stepped
Back into the world of gravity, in silence.

English

THE ART OF COURTESAN
—Anon

I shall instruct you in lessons hierarchic
Passed on to me by my grandma, who had them from
her grandma
Who had received them from her grandma of the fourth
generation preceding.
Leaving out none of them I shall
Teach you all in the order of the Gurus.

The great grandma advised my grandma in secrecy
She in turn transferred them to my mother
Who practiced them and narrated
The same art to me. I shall
Disclose them to you in the order of the Gurus.

Darling, with a voice sweet as the veena and the cuckoo!
Womenfolk should amass as much wealth as possible
From their lovers when their youth is fresh
Thereafter they may live on
Only with their fallen breasts.

For a damsel with a rich bosom
Luxuriant hair, a sweet face
And radiant teeth flashing a smile
The pursuit of wealth is the real pursuit
Yet for that pursuit to bear fruit
Grandma's eyes should keep a watch.

When your eyes blackened and forehead adorned
After offering flowers to God
Wearing ornaments and chewing betel leaves
Go forth, with your maids
To face your crowded lovers with grace.

At the parlour you smile at one of them;
Accost another with a twist of your eyebrows, my daughter
Greet the third with a lowering of the brow
Welcome all others with your glances.

Inside the parlour, O pretty one!
Smile at one, flicker the eyebrows at another
Cast a sidelong glance at one, and nod at the others
Keep the world of lovers thus entertained.

Inside the parlour
Enchant everyone with the corners of your eyes
Making each of them feel you glance at him
Hovering like bees over a myriad lotuses.

Inside the parlour, O pretty one
With your versatile art of entertainment
Rouse desire in the mind of each
And perform to suit their varied whims,
So that they come again, once having gone.
Treat the visiting travellers with civility
Share pleasing secrecies with the lovers
Entertain the poets with betel leaves
Bow before the Brahmins; humour the lustful
Try to allure the high-born
Entice the family men
And blatantly flatter the capricious.

Grasp those who are sincere in love
Ensnare the noble ones with a show of affection
Win over the poets with a display of passion
Give food and clothes to maids
Respect greatly the man useful in future
Take you my counsel, my daughter.

Charm the celibate ones with words, the friends
The dependents with gifts

The family men with affected indignation
The lovers with bewitching glances
The foolish ones with tears of joy
The king with enticing charms
The sensualists with tact
The noble ones with a magic potion
The poets by lending your ears to their verses
And your own relations in other ways.

Translated from Malayalam by P. Narayana

THE BATTLEFIELD
—Kakkaipatiniyar Naccellaiyar

On the weak, shriveled arms of the old woman,
the veins stand out; her stomach is gnarled
as a blade of lotus. Unnerved by the fighting,
her son had turned his back on it. So folks whispered.
If he had fled in the heat of battle,
she thundered in a rage, these breasts that nursed him
I'll tear into pieces. Sword in hand,
she groped around in the bloodstained field,
turning over one lifeless body
after another. When she found her son
lying prostrate, hacked to death,
she rejoiced more than on the day he was born.

Translated from Tamil by R. Parthasarthy

THE CORPSE
—J.P. Das

Someone's lifeless body lies in the street
surrounded by people.
Many simply walk past,
others cannot bear to look at it;
one's step falters, another falls silent,
and another shuts his eyes at the sight.

One passes by reciting mantras along the street;
for whom did this child pluck flowers?
Who laughed here,
who stretched out his arms
to put a halt to time,
and whose screams were lost
in the deserted street?

In the light's rush upstream,
someone was lost on the way; the heart's
many dreams were ground to ash.
Someone sighs deeply,
someone measures out life
with a burning candle,
and another finds his own way
in the half-light.

The people have all gone;
the street is deserted, laughter extinguished
in the end endlessness of space.
The corpse still lies in the middle of the street,
and I lie fast asleep on a lonely isle.

Translated from Oriya by Jayanta Mahapatra

THE COWHERD'S DAUGHTER
—Rūpa Gosvāmin

Oh friend, you
play in the mud like a child
your blouse not
even covering your breasts
your father, the cowherd
thinking you still a child
has done nothing
to find you a husband
but then suddenly
your eyelids leap as you hear
in the Vrindā forest the sound
of Krishna's flute
and you tremble with longing
and show the whites of your eyes.

Translated from Sanskrit by W. S. Merwin and J.M. Masson

THE DIFFERENCE
—Akhtar-ul-Iman

How much I wept when I first realized
that someday I'll die and lose
the delight of all my pleasures,
even the ordinary ones:
pleasures like the hum of bees buzzing,
birds chirping, ravens weaving
straw nests in neem treetops,
tractor engines chugging along,
children playing in the dust,
and half-naked workers chewing on
dry pieces of bread and raw onions.
All these meaningless, ordinary joys
will suddenly vanish.
How much I wept when I first
felt this fear that my ties to the earth
will disappear, and I'll become
lifeless as stone.
But for a long time now my lips
have forgotten how to kiss,
and the exciting tumult of the heart
is a thing of the past,
causing in me this state of perpetual death.
And yet, my eyes haven't shed
even a single tear.

Transcreated from Urdu by Abhay K. and Bill Wolak

THE EVENING
—Garikapati Pavan Kumar

Trees
black as mascara-touched
eyebrows of the beloved

the hill
sliding silently into
deep meditation

the sky
smiling with flushed cheeks.

That evening

in my room
engrossed in my work
with the loneliness
that has become a habit

like a prisoner

only the circling birds
feel happy...

Translated from Telugu by D. Kesava Rao

THE GLOW-WORM'S GLEAM
—Narain Shyam

There is a gleam of the glow-worm,
The night is dark and the journey long.
Light takes one step and darkness another
    There is a gleam of the glow-worm,
    The night is dark and the journey long.
Now here and now there,
flashes of light emanate.
    There is a gleam of the glow-worm,
    The night is dark and the journey long.
This light falls drop by drop but darkness
is a thirst.
    There is a gleam of the glow-worm,
    The night is dark and the journey long.
As you glance, now it glows and now it dies,
But the path darkens more and more,
    There is a gleam of the glow-worm,
    The night is dark and the journey long.
Perhaps one may complete this life's
pilgrimage only thus.
    There is a gleam of the glow-worm,
    The night is dark and the journey long.

Translated from Sindhi by D.K. Mansharamani

THE INSANE
—Vinda Karandikar

She slept with a cloud: and then, of course, she conceived;
The rest followed smoothly. The earthen pitcher at home
She smashed pleasurably and started on a body-ending
pilgrimage.
On her way she met an ass whom she worshipped
ceremoniously.
The left-over of the incense pot she secured greedily and said,
'If this too had turned into ashes what could I say to the world?
But Fate is overwhelming and walks ahead like a dog.'
Then she took some banyan leaves,
      and set them up on a peepal tree.
And said, 'Now I owe nothing to any man,
      not even as much as a full moon.'
The rest followed smoothly (This I mentioned earlier);
The Insane delivered a lightning;
      offering her breast to the lightning,
The Insane went ahead; on her way she met the Court Jester;
Then the King; then the Queen; then A; then B.
But the Insane was sane enough—   she recognized none.

Translated from Marathi by the Poet

THE NEED TO TRAVEL
—Sohini Basak

I cannot rhyme the green bird by my window
with the fan whirling, and my thoughts going backwards
in cycles homewards again. The few rooms that have been mine
I know by heart down to the turtle-shaped smudge
on the mirror, inspiration gathers like dust under the bed
saturated I wait for the night to fall. A screech of an owl
might tear it open, but the moon within the branches
is trapped in clichés. I confess my mind is a boomerang
that's fixed to a vocabulary of the familiar. Pinned
to my wall is the poetry of departures.
I should pack my bags now.

English

THE NEW MAN
—Anon Baul

Come, he greets you now.
The new man
has exchanged his possessions
for the knapsack
of a penniless rover.
Even as he dips into the Ganges
the name of Kali is on his lips.

A simple word
can shatter ignorance and disbelief:
Kali and Krishna are One.
The words are different
their meaning the same.
Breaker of word barriers
he truly
is borderless:
Allah, Jesus, Moses, Kali,
tycoon or pauper
the new man sees them One and the same.

Adrift in his heavenly musings
people take him for a lunatic.
He opens his arms wide
to embrace the world, calling all
to the ferryboat that's moored to life's shore.

Translated by Anon

THE ORIENTALIST
—Ranjit Hoskote

He went back to drafting policies of state
but never forgot the courtesan in the Sanskrit play.
She wrote him letters on pages folded
in triangles like betel leaves
but did not wait for the beloved and spring;
creepers soothed her, her lamp-lit hours passed
among the scented shadows of lovers.

English

THE SLEEP
—Shankha Ghosh

When the sky washed clean the earth's face in the dark of night
None of us knew, we were all asleep.
When the grass blades danced with glee, holding each other
by waist
None of us knew, we were all asleep.
Rain did not descend within our deep sleep
Nor did we descend into the midst of rain. How then
Did the night's solitude, night's silence pass
And the languor of idle morning rise
Before our eyes...

None of us knew, we were all asleep.

Translated from Bengali by Kalyan Roy

THE WAY
—Bodhidharma

Earthlings while enjoying breath
worry themselves about death,
when replete they worry
have they enough to eat:
Great Uncertainty.
The past does not interest the sage,
who cares what comes in some future age.
Even the present cannot hold sway:
from second to second he follows the Way.

Transcreated from Sanskrit by Gabriel Rosenstock

THEY BURNT MY FATHER AND GRANDFATHER
—K. Siva Reddy

They burnt my father and my grandfather
just next to this dust track.
Perhaps they burnt all the dead people in the village
just next to this dust track.
When we go along the dust track
we can still find broken pots, old winnowing baskets
and shrouds on the nearby date-palm trees.

Coming this far
after so long
it's become impossible not to shoulder a cremation ground.
If I wish to shift the burden on to another
he too is shouldering a cremation ground—
I am searching for one who hasn't turned into a cremation
ground.

Translated from Telugu by M. Sridhar and Alladi Uma

THIRST
—Sahir Ludhianvi

World of palaces, crowns and thrones,
What does society care for this day?
A world that measures all that it owns:
What's this world should it come my way?

Injured body, thirsty soul,
Restless glance, the heart afraid,
What world is this? A senseless hole:
What's this world should it come my way?

Playing with people like some wooden toy
Is it life we worship...or is it the grave?
Is it sorrow we seek...or maybe pure joy:
What's this world should it come my way?

Wandering youth in search of hope,
So many bodies up for sale,
Love exchanged for a measly grope:
What's this world should it come my way?

World where man is no more than dust
Loyalty nothing, friendship a game
Love melts so easily into lust:
What's this world should it come my way?

Burn it all on a funeral pyre
Remove this world from me in a blaze
Set it on fire, set it on fire:
What's this world should it come my way?

Transcreated from Urdu by Gabriel Rosenstock

THINGS OF BEAUTY
—Amrita Nair

I cannot do
Any of those beautiful things
Like ikebana
Or origami
Or embroidery.
But that's all right.
Because
I'm good at
Running into these same
Invisible walls
Repeatedly;
Because
There is nothing in this world
Half as beautiful
As a soul that hurtles
Towards
Its own shattering.

English

THIS HELPLESSNESS
—Shamsher Bahadur Singh

This helplessness
    sometimes becomes moon
    sometimes black palm
    a wall, a dam
    a flash of lightning that
    seems to caress the mountain every moment.

This helplessness
    turns simple living
    into a storm of blood.
This helplessness
    is fathomless
    even in silence.

Emotions become a cross
    raised as shoulders
    unbending.
    The joints of bones
    are loosening.
Tears break out of the dreams of lightning:
the earth is dry as the eye.

In the disturbed depths is immense
    silence.

Translated from Hindi by Nalini Taneja

TIBET
—Uday Prakash

Having come from Tibet,
Lamas keep wandering around
These days, mumbling mantras

Their herds of mules
Go down into the gardens
They do not eat marigold flowers

How many flowers
On one marigold plant,
Papa?

When it's the rainy season
in Tibet,
What season
Do we have?

When it's three o'clock
In Tibet,
What time
Is it here?

In Tibet
Are there marigolds,
Papa?

Do lamas blow conch shells, Papa?

Papa,
Have you ever seen lamas
Wrapped in blankets
Running quickly
In the darkness?

When people die
Lamas stand
On all four sides of the graves
And bow their heads

They do not recite mantras.

They whisper—tibbut
tibbut tibbut
tibbut tibbut
tibbut tibbut
And they cry
all night long.

Do lamas
Cry just
Like us, Papa?

Translated from Hindi by Robert A. Hueckstedt

TIME
—Kambadasan

The flame of the bed-chamber lamp
turned red like a newt's tail,
trembled before the rushing breeze
The book slipped from my hands,
I hastened to close the window
Out in the sky
in the poison-black night
countless stars
throbbed with light
Inwardly I trembled
like a trapped fish.
I was all ears
electrified by flute-music
Sweet desire welled up
and touched
my inmost being
like a prisoner bound
like a bee intent on honey
I followed the music's trail
to reach
that daunting crematorium
where I saw
the lone figure of man
As he poured forth
melodies from his flute,
a hooded serpent appeared.
Terrified I cried,
'Look, a deadly snake!'

Was he deaf?
He never moved but
flooded the world

with music from the flute
through his pining breath
All my mounting fears
vanished without a trace
As the first streak of dawn
oozed like milk
from the black pot of night,
I gazed upon his countenance.
Lo! he was blind—
I blind to the world
But he
like a dark cloud,
moved on, raining music
all the way.

Translated from Tamil by N.V. Rajamani

TO HER BESTIES
—Vidyā

How lucky you're all that you recall
the games you played with your lovers,
those moans and laughter, syllables of sweet pain
When my lover unknotted my dress
I swear I remember nothing afterwards.

Translated from Sanskrit by Abhay K.

WHAT BLUE IS
—Binoy Majumdar

I do not swallow my miracle flower in an instant
Like chocolate, I suck it slowly for pleasure
Forgetting my age-old thirst in discovery and love.
I have reflected, with many snakebites on my heart,
Known what it is to be rent apart, what blue is—
In the sky, in the heart; what an impassive bird is.
Or the dragonfly soars on its transparent wings.
Its breath still warm on the young man's heart.
Illness enchants me, I watch the scene at the window
Where the sky drools in the shelter of the wind.
I am entranced, you've flown away; come back, wheel
As the chariot, as victory, as eternal poetry.
We will sing in a pure land, we will be love,
As faceless melody, we will daub all the skies.

Translated from Bengali by Arunava Sinha

WHAT FRENZY IS THIS?
—Zareef Ahmed Zareef

My gaze has been silenced
What frenzy is this?
I lost the city of love I'd found,
What frenzy is this?

I worshiped shadows all my life
Did I alone miss
the arrival of the dawn
What frenzy is this?

I smeared the glass with blood
to make mirrors
My image—a stranger
What frenzy is this?

I couldn't read
the writing on floral walls
my lines of fate turned mute
What frenzy is this?

Socrates did me no favour in leaving
I shouldn't be saying this, but
He didn't drink my share of poison
What frenzy is this?

I've lost the city of love I'd found,
What frenzy is this
My gaze has been silenced
What frenzy is this?

Translated from Kashmiri by the poet

WHEN IT RAINS IN DHARAMSHALA
—Tenzin Tsundue

When it rains in Dharamshala
raindrops wear boxing gloves,
thousands of them
come crashing down
and beat my room.
Under its tin roof
my room cries from inside
and wets my bed, my papers.
Sometimes the clever rain comes
from behind my room,
the treacherous walls lift
their heels and allow
a small flood into my room.
I sit on my island-nation bed
and watch my country in flood,
notes on freedom,
memoirs of my prison days,
letters from college friends,
crumbs of bread
and Maggi noodles
rise sprightly to the surface
like a sudden recovery
of a forgotten memory.
Three months of torture,
monsoon in the needle-leafed pines
Himalaya rinsed clean
glistens in the evening sun.
Until the rain calms down
and stops beating my room
I need to console my tin roof
who has been on duty
from the British Raj.

This room has sheltered
many homeless people.
Now captured by mongooses
and mice, lizards and spiders,
and partly rented by me.
A rented room for home
is a humbling existence.
My Kashmiri landlady
at eighty cannot return home.
We often compete for beauty
Kashmir or Tibet.
Every evening,
I return to my rented room;
but I am not going to die this way.
There has got to be
some way out of here.
I cannot cry like my room
I have cried enough
in prisons and
in small moments of despair.
There has got to be
some way out of here.
I cannot cry,
my room is wet enough.

English

WHILE I SLEPT
—Navtej Bharati

Time aged me
while I slept
I will not forgive it
for this treachery
I will not accept this old age
grafted slyly on my body
I will hide in the
leaves of grass
in the drops of water.
Will slip away
from its wrinkled hands.

Translated from Punjabi by the poet

WHIRLWIND
—Ravji Patel

When I'd finished my bath
I wiped my body
with the smell of the green fields.

The moment I whistled,
cows jumped in
through the window
carrying the morning's sunshine
on their horns,

buffaloes jumped in
their bodies slick
with the waters of the lake
foul with fish-smells,

goats jumped in
with lonely roads,
the muddy edges of roads
deserted fields
and peacock feathers
in their eyes,

I jumped in,
a whirlwind in the house.

Translated from Gujarati by Hansa Jhaveri

WHY MARRY?
—Vemana

Why would you marry, have children,
call woes down upon yourself?

It defies logic—

Like hoisting
a boulder
from the earth
   to bear
   upon
   your
   head.

We know all about it when a rich man has a rash,
but whoever hears about a poor man's nuptials?

Transcreated from Telugu by Amanda Bell

WINTER
—Bijoy Sankar Barman

Shrouded in fog
is the distant red hillock
A tree
leans over the river

Canoes glide over the rapids
Night buries the sighs of dusk

In the lonely house
emptied by the last autumn wind
an old violin has so long remained
covered in dust

Last night
after the rain I saw
a shadow lying by my head
on the floor

Was it mine

Translated from Assamese by Nirendra Nath Thakuria

YOU ARE THAT
from the *Chhandogya Upanishad* VI. I2. 1-3

Uddalaka asked his son to fetch a banyan fruit.

'Here it is, Lord!' said Svetaketu.
'Break it,' said Uddalaka.
'I have broken it, Lord!'
'What do you see there?'
'Little seeds, Lord!'
'Break one of them, my son!'
'It is broken, Lord!'
'What do you see there?'
'Nothing Lord!' said Svetaketu.
Uddalaka said: 'My son! This great banyan tree
has sprung up from seed so small
that you cannot see it.
Believe in what I say, my son!
That being is the seed; all else
but His expression.
He is truth. He is Self.
Svetaketu! You are that.'

Translated from Sanskrit by Shree Purohit Swami and W.B. Yeats

YOUR THOUGHTS
—Raghuvir Sahay

How confidently you express my thoughts, even if inaccurately!
I never had the self-assurance to do so,
even when I hoped I might be right.
I never raised my voice—assumed that the right
to do so was mine alone, but lacking thoughts of your own
you have stolen mine,
and how authoritatively you trumpet them!
I suppress a little grin, try to conceal my amusement from you,
so as to save my thoughts from your misrepresentation.
I keep them to myself, for my own expression—
let you lose yourself down some blind alley.

Transcreated from Hindi by Amanda Bell

YOUR TRUST
—Om Nagar

How fast collapses
your trust
like a pack of cards

If I had met you at the grocery shop
I would have put two handfuls of trust long ago
in your wounded palms

like sand castles
your trust collapses
as soon as I withdraw my feet

you throw in the sky with your hands
walls, verandahs and those little windows
where you place an earthen lamp every night to light up inside

sometimes your trust perches on the top of date-palms
and I start digging shadows,
deeper I dig, deeper the trust grows.

Translated from Rajasthani by Abhay K.

ACKNOWLEDGEMENTS

I express my gratitude to Shelly Bhoil for her minute observations and valuable suggestions.

I want to thank my lovely wife Ekaterina and daughter Kaya for their love and support during completion of this labour of love. I take full responsibility for any inadvertent error which may have crept in the anthology.

PERMISSIONS ACKNOWLEDGMENTS

All the poems included in the anthology have been voluntarily contributed by the poets and their translators. Permission to include the poems has been granted by the individual poets, translators and publishers. If, through inability to trace the present copyright owners, any copyright material is included for which permission has not specifically been sought, apologies are tendered in advance to proprietors and publishers concerned.

'After the Curfew' by Nida Fazli, translated from Urdu by Nirupama Dutt, used by permission of Nirupama Dutt.

'Again Snowfall' by Jiban Namdung, translated from Nepali by Jas Yonjan 'Pyasi'.

'A Love Poem from India: Author's Consent' by Mahe Jabeen, translated from Telugu by Velcheru Narayan Rao, used by permission of Mahe Jabeen and Velcheru Narayan Rao.

'Alphabets' by Nabaneeta Dev Sen, translated from Bengali by Nandana Sen, used by permission of Nabaneeta Dev Sen and Nandana Sen.

'A Marvel' by Anon, translated from Sanskrit by W.S. Merwin and J.M. Masson, used by permission of J.M. Masson.

'And Death Demands a Labor' by Sumita Chakraborty, used by permission of Sumita Chakraborty.

'A New Way of Waiting' by Shakunt Mathur, translated from Hindi by Aruna Sitesh and Arlene Zide, used by permission of Arlene Zide.

'An Asian Child Enters a British Classroom' by Debjani Chatterjee, previously published in Debjani Chatterjee's collection *Do You Hear the Storm Sing?* (Core Publications, London, 2014), used by permission of Debjani Chatterjee.

'An Invitation' by Vallana, transcreated from Sanskrit by Amanda Bell, used by permission of Amanda Bell.

'An Orange' by Jibananada Das, translated from Bengali by Arunava Sinha, used by permission of Arunava Sinha.

'Apparition on the River Bank' by Bhojya Deva transcreated from Sanskrit by by Bill Wolak, used by permission of Bill Wolak.

'God' by Anuradha Mahapatra, transcreation from Bengali by Bill Wolak, used by permission of Bill Wolak.

'Here Comes God' by Tenetti Suri, translated from Telugu by Velcheru Narayan Rao, used by permission of Velcheru Narayan Rao.

'History of Justice' by Rohan Chhetri, used by permission of Rohan Chhetri.

'How can a River Reject its Fish' by Janabai, transcreated from Marathi by Bill Wolak, used by permission of Bill Wolak.

'Ice Cubes, Cake & Roti' by Souvik Bandopadhyay, translated from Bengali by Neelav Bose, first appeared in the journal of the Poetry Society of India vol. 23, 2012, used by permission of Souvik Bandopadhyay and Neelav Bose.

'I have Brought the Sacrificial Goat' by Joy Goswami. From *Selected Poems: Joy Goswami* translated from Bengali by Sampurna Chattarji (Harper Perennial, 2014). Used by permission of Sampurna Chattarji.

'Imaginary Number' by Vijay Seshadri, used by permission of Vijay Seshadri.

'Incurable by Yaquin', translated from Urdu by Edward Powys Mathers, available in public domain.

'In the Dust Forever' by Tarannum Riyaz, translated from Urdu by Miraan Punjabi, used by permission of Tarannum Riyaz.

'In the Event of Change' by Tsering Wangmo Dhompa, used by permission of Tsering Wangmo Dhompa.

'I Wear My Wordlessness' by K. Srilata, used by permission of K. Srilata.

'Jaisalmer – IV' by Gulammohamed Sheikh, translated from Gujarati by the poet and Adil Jussawala, used by permission of Gulammohamed Sheikh and Adil Jussawala.

'Let Loose the Stinging Bees' by Kanji Patel, translated from Gujarati by Gopika Jadeja, used by permission of Gopika Jadeja.

'Lineage' by Attoor Raviverma, translated from Malayalam by K. Satchidanandan, used by permission of Attoor Raviverma and K. Satchidanandan.

'Love is Renewed with Every Breath' by Bulleh Shah, translated from Punjabi by K.S. Duggal.

'Making Love to Her' by Dharmakirti from *Subhashit Ratnakosha* (477), translated from Sanskrit by Abhay K., used by permission of Abhay K.

'Meditations on Desire' by Saleem Peeradina, used by permission of Saleem Peeradina.

'Momin' by Kailash Vajpeyi, translated from Hindi by Ananya Vajpeyi, used by permission of Ananya Vajpeyi.

'Monsoon Poem' by Tishani Doshi, first published in *Girls are Coming out of the Woods* (Harper Collins), used by permission of Tishani Doshi.

'Mountain Child' by Nirmala Putul, translated from Hindi by Lucy Rosenstein, used by permission of Lucy Rosenstein.

'My Eight-anna Coin' by Vinod Kumar Shukla, translated from Hindi by Arvind Krishna Mehrotra, used by permission of Vinod Kumar Shukla and Arvind Krishna Mehrotra.

'My Sister's Bible' by S. Joseph, translated from Malayalam by K. Satchidanandan, used by permission of S. Joseph and K. Satchidanandan.

'Need' by Ramesh Chandra Shah, translated from Hindi by the poet.

'Negro, My Brother' by Ali Sardar Jafri, translated from Urdu by Baider Bakht and Kathleen Grant Jaeger.

'Night's Golden Wineglasses' by Habba Khatoon, transcreated from Kashmiri by Abhay K. and Bill Wolak, used by permission of Abhay K. and Bill Wolak.

'No, I Am not Losing My Sleep' by Pash, translated from Punjabi by Suresh Sethi.

'Only a Connoisseur' by Anon.

'Only One Face' by Pankaj Chaturvedi, translated from Hindi by Rahul Soni, used by permission of Pankaj Chaturvedi and Rahul Soni.

'Pigeons' by Bibhu Padhi, used by permission of Bibhu Padhi.

'Portrait' by Dinkar Manwar, translated from Marathi by Sachin Ketkar, used by permission of Dinkar Manwar and Sachin Ketkar.

'Prayer' by Prabodh Parikh, translated from Gujarati by Naushil Mehta and Ranjit Hoskote, used by permission of Prabodh Parikh and Ranjit Hoskote.

Rāghavapāṇḍavīya 1.47 by Kavirāja, transcreated from Sanskrit by Gabriel Rosenstock and Abhay K., used by permission of Gabriel Rosenstock and Abhay K.

'Rumi and the Reed' by Tabish Khair, used by permission of Tabish Khair.

'Satyabhama' by Basudev Sunani, translated from Odia by Rabindra K. Swain, used by permission of Basudev Sunani and Rabindra K. Swain.

'Shadow' by Brij Nath Betab, translated from Kashmiri by the poet, used by permission of Brij Nath Betab.

'Silhouette' by Adil Jussawala, used by permission of Adil Jussawala.

'Sita's Tears' by Udayan Vajpeyi, translated from Hindi by Alok Bhalla, used by permission of Alok Bhalla.

'Son to Mother' by Gnanakoothan, translated from Tamil by Ashokamitran.

'Summer Afternoon' by Vijay Deo Narayan Shahi, translated from Hindi by Arvind Krishna Mehrotra, used by permission of Arvind Krishna Mehrotra.

'Terms of Seeing' by E. V. Ramakrishnan, used by permission of E. V. Ramakrishnan.

'The Art of Courtesan' by Anon, translated from Malayalam by P. Narayana.

'The Battlefield' (Purananuru 278) by Kakkaipatiniyar Naccellaiyar, translated from Tamil by R. Parthasarathy, used by permission of R. Parthasarathy.

'The Corpse' by J.P. Das, translated from Odia by Jayanta Mahapatra, used by permission of J.P. Das and Jayanata Mahapatra.

'The Cowherd's Daughter' by Rūpa Gosvāmin, translated from Sanskrit by W. S. Merwin & J.M. Masson, used by permission of J.M. Masson.

'The Difference' by Akhtar-ul-Iman, transcreated from Urdu by Abhay K. and Bill Wolak, used by permission of Abhay K. and Bill Wolak.

'The Glow-Worm's Gleam' by Narain Shyam, translated from Sindhi by D.K. Mansharamani.

'The Evening' by Garikapati Pavan Kumar, translated from Telugu by D. Kesava Rao.

'The Insane' by Vinda Karandikar, translated from Marathi by the poet.

'The Need to Travel' by Sohini Basak, used by permission of Sohini Basak.

'The New Man' by Anon Baul.

'The Orientalist' by Ranjit Hoskote, first published in Ranjit Hoskote, *Vanishing Acts: New & Selected Poems 1985-2005* (New Delhi: Penguin, 2006) used by permission of Ranjit Hoskote.

'The Sleep' by Sankha Ghosh, translated from Bengali by Kalyan Roy.

'The Way' by Bodhidharma, transcreated from Sanskrit by Gabriel Rosenstock, used by permission of Gabriel Rosenstock.

'They Burnt My Father and Grandfather' by K. Siva Reddy, translated from Telugu by M. Sridhar and Alladi Uma, used by permission of K. Siva Reddy, M. Sridhar and Alladi Uma.

'Thirst' by Sahir Ludhianvi, transcreated from Urdu by Gabriel Rosenstock, used by permission of Gabriel Rosenstock.

'Things of Beauty' by Amrita Nair, used by permission of Amrita Nair.

'This Helplessness' by Shamsher Bahadur Singh, translated from Hindi by Nalini Taneja, used by permission of Nalini Taneja.

'Tibet' by Uday Prakash, translated from Hindi by Robert A. Hueckstedt, used by permission of Uday Prakash and Robert A. Hueckstedt.

'Time' by Kambadasan, translated from Tamil by N.V. Rajamani

'To Her Besties' by Vidyā, translated from Sanskrit by Abhay K., used by permission of Abhay K.

'What Frenzy is this?' by Zareef Ahmed Zareef, translated from Kashmiri by the poet, used by permission of Zareef Ahmed Zareef.

'What Blue Is' by Binoy Majumdar from *Come Back Wheel (No. 70)*, translated from Bengali by Arunava Sinha, used by permission of Arunava Sinha.

'When it Rains in Dharamshala' by Tenzin Tsundue, used by permission of Tenzin Tsundue.

'Whirlwind' by Ravji Patel translated from Gujarati by Hansa Jhaveri.

'Why Marry' by Vemana, transcreated from Telugu by Amanda Bell, used by permission of Amanda Bell.

'Winter' by Bijoy Sankar Barman, translated from Assamese by Narendra Nath Thakuria, used by permission of Bijoy Sankar Barman and Narendra Nath Thakuria.

'You are That' from *Chhandogya Upanishad*, translated from Sanskrit by Swami Purohit and W.B. Yeats, in public domain.

'Your Thoughts' by Raghuvir Sahay, transcreated from Hindi by Amanda Bell, used by permission of Amanda Bell.

'Your Trust' by Om Nagar translated from Rajasthani by Abhay K. used by permission of Om Nagar and Abhay K.

POETS

Adil Jussawala (b. 1940) is the author of four books of poems. His third book, *Trying to Say Goodbye*, was given a Sahitya Akademi award in 2014. He has been a language teacher, a lecturer, and literary editor and columnist for several newspapers and magazines.

Akhtar-ul-Iman (1915–1996) is a poet, scholar, film script writer and director. He wrote in Urdu, published eight collections of poetry and received Sahitya Akademi Award.

Ali Sardar Jafri (1913–2000) is a prolific and versatile Urdu writer, poet, critic and film lyricist. He received Jnanpith Award in 1997 and Padma Shri in 1967.

Alok Dhanwa (b. 1948) is poet from Munger, Bihar who has been active in the left cultural movement since decades. He has two poetry collections to his credit. He has received several awards including Rahul Samman and Bihar Rashtrabhasa Parishad Award.

Amit Majmudar (b. 1979) is poet and novelist, translator, essayist, and diagnostic nuclear radiologist (M.D.) who lives in Ohio, USA. His latest book is *Godsong*: A Verse Translation of the *Bhagvad-Gita* with commentary.

Amrita V. Nair (b. 1989) is a writer based in Singapore. Her first collection of poetry, *Yours Affectionately*, was published in 2009 and received the Jury's commendation at the Muse India National Literary Awards 2011.

Angshuman Kar (b. 1975) is the author of nine collections of poems, two novels, two novellas and a memoir. He received several awards, including the Krittibas Award in 2007.

Annamayya (1408–1503) is a Hindu saint and the earliest known Indian musician to compose songs called *sankirtanas* in praise of the god Venkateswara, a form of Vishnu.

Anuradha Mahapatra (b. 1957) is a poet, writer and social activist. She writes in Bengali. She has published four collections of poems and two collections of essays.

Attoor Ravi Varma (b. 1930) is one of the pioneers of modern Malayalam poetry, who has won the Kendriya Sahitya Akademi Award for his contributions to literary world.

Basudev Sunani (b. 1962) is the author of four poetry collections. He is considered as a significant Dalit voice in Odia poetry.

Bhojya Deva is a well-known 11th century poet, patron of poets and King of Dhara.

Bibhu Padhi (b. 1951) has published eleven books of poetry. His poems have appeared in distinguished magazines and anthologies throughout the English-speaking world.

Bijoy Sankar Barman (b. 1980) is an Assamese poet and translator with ten published books to his credit. He received Sahitya Akademi Yuva Puraskar in 2013 among other awards.

Binoy Majumdar (1934–2006) is a prominent Bengali poet. He published seven poetry collections and received several awards including the Sahitya Akademi Award in 2005.

Bodhidharma (5th-6th century CE) is a Buddhist monk traditionally credited as the transmitter of Chan Buddhism to China. According to Chinese legend, he also began the physical training of the monks of Shaolin Monastery creating Shaolin kungfu.

Brij Nath Betab (b. 1953) is a renowned Kashmiri poet and an important voice in Kashmiri poetry in post independent India. His poems sing the pain of exile from the homeland. He has been honoured with several awards including Delhi State Urdu Academy Award.

Buddhadev Bose (1908–1974) is a major voice in Bengali literature. He wrote novels, short stories, plays and essays in addition to poetry. He received Sahitya Akademi Award in 1967 and Padma Bhusan in 1970.

Bulleh Shah (1680–1757) is a Punjabi poet and philosopher. His first spiritual teacher was Shah Inayat Qadiri, a Sufi murshid of Lahore. The verse form Bulleh Shah primarily employed is the Kafi, popular in Punjabi (Saraiki) and Sindhi poetry.

Debjani Chatterjee (b. 1952) is a poet based in UK. She has written, translated, or edited more than 60 books. She was honoured with an MBE in 2008.

Devara Dasimaya is a 10th century poet who wrote in Kannada. He composed *vachanas* in the name of his god Ramnath.

Dharmakriti is an influential Indian Buddhist philosopher. He was active in the 6-7th century. He worked at Nalanda and was one of the key scholars of epistemology (pramana) in Buddhist philosophy.

Dinkar Manwar (b. 1965) is a poet, editor and artist from Maharashtra, India. His poems have been published in various literary journals and he has two poetry collections to his credit.

E.V. Ramakrishnan (1950) is a bilingual writer and translator. He has published poetry and literary criticism in Malayalam, his mother tongue and English. He has three volumes of poetry in English and five critical books in Malayalam. He received Kerala Sahitya Akademi Award.

Garikapati Pavan Kumar (b. 1972) is a poet and a translator. He has translated poems of Pablo Neruda into Telugu. His first book of poems in Telugu received Ismail Award. He lives in the United States.

Gulam Mohammed Sheikh (1937) is a painter, poet and art critic from Gujarat. He was awarded the Padmashri in 1983 and Padmabhushan in 2014 for his contribution in the field of art.

Habba Khatun (1554–1609) is a 16th century poet and ascetic, who is also known as the 'Nightingale of Kashmir'. She is a legendary figure in Kashmiri literary history.

H.S. Shivaprakash (b. 1954) is a leading Kannada poet and playwright. He has several published anthologies of poems and plays to his credit. He received Sahitya Akademi Award in 2012.

Janabai is a 14th century Marathi poet. She is traditionally attributed with the authorship of about 300 *abhangas*. She is revered as a saint by the followers of Warakari sect in Maharashtra.

Jibanananda Das (1899–1954) is a Bengali poet, writer, novelist and essayist. He is considered the most important voice in Bengali poetry after Tagore. During his lifetime, only seven volumes of his poems were published.

Jiban Narah (b. 1970) is the author of six books of poetry in Assamese. His poems have been translated into many other languages.

Jiwan Namdung (b. 1951) is one of the prominent literary figures in the contemporary Indian Nepali Literature. His significant work of criticism *Paryavekshan* won the Sahitya Akademi Award (1994).

J.P. Das (b. 1936) is a well-known poet, fiction writer and playwright from Odisha. He is the winner of many honours including the Sahitya Akademi Award and the Saraswati Samman.

Kailash Vajpeyi (1936–2015) is a renowned Hindi poet. He received Sahitya Akademi Award in 2009 for his collection of poems *Hawa me Hastakshar.*

Kalpatta Narayanan (b. 1950) is a poet, essayist, novelist and a cultural activist. He writes in Malayalam.

Kambadasan (1916–1973) is an Indian writer, poet and popular film lyricist who worked mainly in Tamil-language films. He wrote several short stories, poems and plays.

Kanji Patel (b. 1952) is a prominent poet-novelist of Gujarat. His published works revolve around folk and Adivasi communities and make use of the Adivasi language. His works have been widely translated.

Kavirāja is a 12th century Sanskrit poet famous for his double meaning poem, the *Rāghavapāṇḍavīya—Story of the Scion of Raghu and the Sons of Pāṇḍu,* the *Rāmāyaṇa* and the *Mahābhārata.*

K. Siva Reddy (b. 1943) is a significant voice in contemporary Telugu poetry. He has published eleven collections of poems and has won several awards including the Sahitya Akademi award in 1990.

K. Srilata (b. 1968) is a Chennai-based poet, fiction writer and translator. She writes in English. She has several publications to her credit.

Mahe Jabeen (b. 1961) is a poet, lawyer and minority rights activist. Her poem features in the anthology *Hibiscus on the Lake: Twentieth-century Telugu Poetry from India* (University of Wisconsin Press).

Manohar Shetty (b. 1953) is a Goa-based poet who has eight books of poems to his credit and is one of the prominent Indian poets writing in the English language.

Meena Alexander (b. 1951) is the author of numerous collections of poetry including *Atmospheric Embroidery* (2018). She has received several awards. She lives in New York City and is distinguished Professor of English at the Graduate Center/Hunter College, CUNY.

Mohammad Alvi (b. 1927) is a Urdu poet and the recipient of the Sahitya Akademi Award (1992). He published four collections of poems.

Nabaneeta Dev Sen (b. 1938) is an award-winning Indian poet, novelist and academic. She received Sahitya Akademi Award in 1999 and Padma Shri in 2000.

Narain Shyam (1922–1989) is a prominent Sindhi poet. He published eleven collections of poetry. He received Sahitya Akademi Award in 1970.

Navtej Bharati (b. 1938) writes poetry and prose in Punjabi and English. His awards include Best Poet of the State (three times: 1959, 1960, 1961) by the Government of Punjab and the Anad Kav Sanman (Delhi, 2010). He lives in Canada.

Nida Fazli (1938–2016) is a prominent poet, lyricist and dialogue writer in Hindi and Urdu. He was awarded the Padma Shri in 2013 for his contribution to literature.

Niranjan Chakma (b. 1951) has published eight collections of poetry. He received Ambedkar Fellowship Award in 1997. He lives in Agartala.

Nirmala Putul (b. 1972) writes in the Indian tribal language, Santali. A collection of her poems *Nagare Ki Tarah Bajte Hain Shabad* (Words resound like drums) was published in 2004. She counterpoises her tribal world with the 'developed' modern world.

Om Nagar (b. 1980) is the recipient of Sahitya Akademi's Yuva Purashkar 2012 for his collection of poems in Rajasthani. He has published four poetry collections. His poems have been translated into several Indian languages.

Padma Sachdev (b. 1940) is a poet and novelist. She is the first modern woman poet of the Dogri language. She also writes in Hindi and has published several poetry collections. She won the Sahitya Akademi Award in 1971.

Pankaj Chaturvedi (b. 1971) is a Hindi poet and critic. He has two poetry collections to his credit and has received Bharat Bhusan Samman Agrawal Samman and Devishankar Awasthi Samman.

Pash (1950–1988) is the pen name of Avtar Singh Sandhu. He was a major poet of the Naxalite movement in the Punjabi literature in 1970s.

Raghuvir Sahay (1929–1990) is a versatile Hindi poet, short-story writer, essayist, literary critic, translator, and journalist. He worked as the chief-editor of noted Hindi weekly, Dinmaan from 1969–82. He received the 1984 Sahitya Akademi Award.

Ramesh Chandra Shah (b. 1937) is a poet, novelist and critic. He received Sahitya Akademi Award for his novel, Vinayak in 2014.

He was also conferred Padma Shri, the fourth highest Indian civilian award in 2004.

Ranjit Hoskote (b.1969) is the author of six collections of poetry. He has received the Sahitya Akademi Golden Jubilee Award, the Sahitya Akademi Translation Award, and the S H Raza Award for Literature.

Ravi Shankar (b. 1975) is an Indian American poet, editor, and former literature professor at Central Connecticut State University. He received a Pushcart prize and has several collections of poetry to his credit.

Ravji Patel (1939–1968) is a poet, short story writer and novelist. He wrote in Gujarati. His only poetry collection *Angat* (1970) was published posthumously. It includes fourteen songs.

Rohan Chhetri (b. 1987) won 'Emerging Poets Prize 2015' for his first book of poems, *Slow Startle*. His poems have been published in several literary journals and have been translated into French. He was a 2016 Norman Mailer Poetry Fellow.

Rupa Goswamin (1489–1564) is a poet, philosopher and Guru of the Gaudiya Vaishnava tradition. He wrote a number of texts in Sanskrit on philosophy, poetics, drama and dramaturgy.

Sahir Ludhyanvi (1921-1980) is the pen name of poet and lyricist Abdul Hayee. He wrote in both in Hindi and Urdu. He won two Filmfare awards and received Padma Shri in 1971.

Saleem Peeradina (b. 1944) is the author of six books of poetry. He is an Emeritus Professor of English at Siena Heights University, Michigan, USA.

Sampurna Chattarji (b. 1970) is a poet, novelist and translator. She has fourteen books to her credit including five poetry collections. Her translation of poems of Joy Goswami was shortlisted for inaugural Khushwant Singh Memorial Prize for Poetry.

Sankha Ghosh (b. 1932) writes in Bengali and has several collections of poems to his credit. He received Sahitya Akademi Award in 1977 and Jnanpith Award in 2016.

Shakunt Mathur (b. 1922) is an experimental Hindi writer who contributed to New Poetry movement in Hindi literature in 1960–70s. She published three collections of poems.

Shamsher Bahadur Singh (1911–1993) was an important voice in progressive school of modern Hindi poetry. He published several

poetry collections and received Sahitya Akademi Award in 1977 and Kabir Samman in 1989.

S. Joseph (b. 1965) writes in Malayalam. He received Kerala Sahitya Akademi Award in 2012. He has a number of poetry collections to his credit.

Sohini Basak's (b. 1991) debut collection of poems *we live in the newness of small differences* received the inaugural Beverley Manuscript Prize. She works as an editor at Harper Collins, India.

Souvik Bandyopadhyay (b. 1975) writes in Bengali. He has seven collections of poetry to his credit and has won several awards for poetry including the prestigious Mallika Sengupta Purashkar in 2017.

Sumita Chakraborty (b. 1987) is poetry editor of AGNI Magazine. She received a Ruth Lilly and Dorothy Sargent Rosenberg Fellowship from the Poetry Foundation in 2017 and was shortlisted for the Forward Prize for Best Single Poem by the Forward Arts Foundation in 2018.

Sunil Gangopadhyay (1934–2012) is a poet and novelist who wrote in Bengali. He received Sahitya Akademi award in 1985 for his novel *Those Days (Sei Samaya)*.

Tabish Khair (b. 1966) is as associate professor at Aarhus University. Winner of the All India Poetry Prize, he is the author of several critically acclaimed novels and the poetry collections, *Where Parallel Lines Meet and Man of Glass*.

Tarannum Riyaz (b. 1953) is a noted Urdu fiction writer, critic, poet, essayist and translator. She has published several books. She received SAARC Literary Award 2014.

Tenetti Suri (1911–1958) is a prominent Telugu poet whose poems have been anthologized in *Hibiscus on the Lake: An Anthology of 20th century Telugu Poetry* edited by Velcheru Narayan Rao.

Tenzin Tsundue (b. 1975) is a poet, writer and an activist working for the Tibetan freedom movement. He has published four books. He won the first Outlook-Picador Award for Non-Fiction.

Tishani Doshi (b. 1975) is an award-winning poet, novelist and dancer. Her most recent book is *Girls Are Coming Out of the Woods*. *Small Days and Nights* is her forthcoming novel. She lives on a beach in Tamil Nadu with her husband and three dogs.

Tsering Wangmo Dhompa was born to Tibetan refugees in India (1969) and is now based in the US. She is the author of three poetry collections including *My Rice Tastes like the Lake* (2011) which was nominated for the Asian American Literary Awards. Her nonfiction book *A Home in Tibet* was published in 2014.

Uday Prakash (b. 1952) is a Hindi poet, scholar, journalist, translator and short story writer from India. He writes for major dailies and periodicals as a freelancer. He received SAARC Literary Award 2009.

Udayan Vajpeyi (b. 1960) is a Hindi poet, essayist, script writer and translator. He has published two volumes of poetry, a short story collection, a book of essays and has received several awards.

Vallana is a well-known Sanskrit poet who is thought to have lived between the 9th and 10th century CE. Several of his poems appear in Vidyakara's poetry anthology *Subhashita Ratnakosa*.

Vasant Abaji Dahake (b. 1942) is a Marathi poet, playwright, short story writer, artist, and critic from Amaravati, Maharashtra. He received Sahitya Akademi Award in 2009 for his collection *Chitralipi*.

Vemana is a 17th century Telugu poet. His poems are known for their use of simple language and native idioms. Vemana's poems were collected and published by C.P. Brown in the 19th century.

Vidya is among the foremost women poets in Sanskrit. Her verses have been included in *Subhashitaratnakosa* of Vidyakara, compiled in the 11th century CE.

Vijay Deo Narayan Shahi (1924–1982) is Hindi poet of repute. He is also known for his essays and literary criticism.

Vijay Seshadri (b. 1954) is a poet, essayist and literary critic. He won the 2014 Pulitzer Prize for poetry for *3 Sections*. His parents immigrated to the United States from Bangalore, India when he was five.

Vinda Karandikar (1918–2010) is a well-known Marathi poet, writer, literary critic, and translator. He translated his own poems into English. He received Jnanpith Award in 2003.

Vinod Kumar Shukla (b. 1937) is a prominent Hindi poet and novelist. He received Sahitya Akademi Award in 1999 for his novel *Deewar Mein Ek Khirkee Rahati Thi* (A Window lived in a Wall).

Yaquin (1727–1755) is a noted Urdu poet who was a rival of poet Mir Taqui Mir. He wrote poetry full of delicate and subtle romantic emotions. He was killed by his own father for unknown reasons.

Zareef Ahmed Zareef (b. 1943) writes poetry in Kashmiri. He has published four collections of poems. He is well-known for his satirical poems.

TRANSLATORS

Ajoy Ranjan Biswas is a poet and a well-known translator from Bengali into English. He retired as a Reader in English from Vivekanand College, Burdwan.

Alladi Uma taught at the University of Hyderabad for twenty years and is a well-known translator from Telugu into English.

Amanda Bell is a poet and translator based in Dublin, Ireland. Her recent publications include a poetry collection, an illustrated children's book, and a collection of haibun and haiku.

Ananya Vajpeyi is an Indian academic and writer. She is the author of the award-winning book *Righteous Republic: The Political foundations of Modern India* (Harvard University Press).

Arlene Zide is a poet and translator based in New York. She translates from Hindi and Urdu.

Arunava Sinha translates classic, modern and contemporary Bengali fiction, non-fiction and poetry from India and Bangladesh into English. Over forty of his translations have been published so far.

Arvind Krishna Mehrotra is a poet, anthologist, literary critic and translator. He is widely recognized for expanding the Indian English language poetry tradition.

Ashokamitran is the pen name of Jagadisa Thyagarajan, who is regarded as one of the most influential figure of Tamil lit of post-indepence era.

Bart Marshall is a well-known translator from Sanskrit into English. He has translated *Ashtavakra Gita* into English.

Bill Wolak is an American poet and translator. He teaches creative writing at William Paterson University in New Jersey.

Bonnie MacDougall teaches at the University of Sydney and is a well-known translator.

David Shulman is an Indologist and regarded as one of the world's foremost authorities on the languages of India.

D. Kesava Rao is a well-known academic and translator from Telugu into English. His translations have appeared in several reputed literary journals.

D.K. Mansharamani is a noted translator. He translates from Sindhi into English.

E. Powys Mathers is an English translator and poet, known for his translation of *Asian Love Poems* and *One Thousand and One Nights*.

Gabriel Rosenstock is a poet, novelist, essayist, playwright, author and translator of over 180 books, mostly in Irish (Gaelic).

Gopika Jadeja is a bi-lingual poet and translator, writing in English and Gujarati. A recipient of the Charles Wallace Scholarship for Creative Writing, her poetry and translations have been published widely.

Jas Yonjan 'Pyasi' is a poet and translator. He writes and translates from Nepali and Bengali.

Jayanta Mahapatra is one of the best known contemporary Indian English poets. He translates from Odia into English.

J.M. Masson is an American author and translator. His translations of Sanskrit poems have received wide praise.

Kalyan Roy translates from Bengali into English.

K. Satchidanandan is a poet and critic. A pioneer of modern poetry in Malayalam, a bilingual literary critic, playwright, editor, columnist and translator from Malayalam into English.

K.S. Duggal is a well-known writer of short stories, novels, dramas and plays. He received Sahitya Akademi Fellowship Award.

Lucy Rosenstein teaches Hindi at SOAS, University of London. She grew up in Bulgaria.

Lyra Neog teaches English literature at Nowgong College, Assam and translates from Assamese into English.

M. Sridhar is former Professor at the Department of English Literature in the University of Hyderabad, India. He has published extensively in the areas of literary theory, comparative literature and translation.

Nalini Taneja is a professor at Delhi University. She translates from Hindi into English.

Nabaneeta Dev Sen is an actor, writer, and child-rights activist. She studied literature at Harvard and has worked as a book editor, a screen writer, a short-film maker and a poetry translator.

Narendranath Thakuria is a well-known translator from Assamese into English. His translations have appeared in Poetry International Web and leading literary journals.

Naushil Mehta is a well-known writer, producer and film director.

Neelav Bose is an occasional translator from Bengali into English.

Nirupama Dutt is a poet, translator, author and literary/art critic based in Chandigarh.

Rabindra K. Swain has five books of poems to his credit. He translates from his mother tongue Odia. He is the managing editor of literary journal *Chandrabhaga*.

Rahul Soni is a well-known writer, translator and editor. He edited an anthology of Hindi Poetry in English translation and translated Shrikant Verma's collection of poetry *Magadh* among others.

Robert A. Hueckstedt teaches Hindi, Urdu and Sanskrit at the University of Virginia. His major interests are kavya, literature, literary theory, and translation.

R. Parthasarathy is a poet, translator, and editor. His translation of the Tamil epic, *The Tale of an Anklet* (Columbia University Press, 1993), received the Sahitya Akademi award in 1996.

Sachin Ketkar is a bilingual writer, translator, editor, blogger and researcher based in Baroda, Gujarat. He won Indian Literature Poetry Translation Prize for translation of modern Gujarati poetry in 2000.

Suresh Sethi is a well-known translator from Punjabi into English. Several of his translations have appeared in *Indian Literature* and other reputed journals.

Udayan Ghosh is a poet and translator from Assam. His translations have been published in several literary journals. He lives in Kolkata.

Velcheru Narayan Rao is a well-known translator from Telugu into English and a professor of Telugu Culture, Literature and History at Emory University, Atlanta, Georgia.

W.S. Merwin is a leading American writer whose poetry, translations, and prose have received accolades.

POETS INDEX